THE CLASH OF GROUP INTERESTS

THE CLASH OF GROUP INTERESTS

Ludwig von Mises

MISES INSTITUTE

Published by Ludwig von Mises Institute
518 West Magnolia Avenue
Auburn, Alabama 36832
Mises.org

Large Print Edition published 2012 by Skyler J. Collins.
Visit: www.skylerjcollins.com

Cover image by StockFreeImages.com.

ISBN-13: 978-1479372980
ISBN-10: 1479372986

Contents

Preface by Murray N. Rothbard   vii

The Clash of Group Interests   1

On Equality and Inequality   27

Index   51

About the Mises Institute   55

PREFACE
MURRAY N. ROTHBARD

IN THE TWENTIETH CENTURY, the advocates of free market economics almost invariably pin the blame for government intervention solely on erroneous ideas—that is, on incorrect ideas about which policies will advance the public weal. To most of these writers, any such concept as "ruling class" sounds impossibly Marxist. In short, what they are really saying is that there are no irreconcilable conflicts of class or group interest in human history, that everyone's interests are always compatible, and that therefore any political clashes can only stem from misapprehensions of this common interest.

In "The Clash of Group Interests," Ludwig von Mises, the outstanding champion of the free market in this century, avoids the naïve trap

This is an abridged version of Rothbard's 1978 preface to Ludwig von Mises's *The Clash of Group Interests and Other Essays*, Occasional Paper Series no. 7, Center for Libertarian Studies monograph.

embraced by so many of his colleagues. Instead, Mises sets forth a highly sophisticated and libertarian theory of classes and of class conflict, by distinguishing sharply between the free market and government intervention. It is true that on the *free market* there are no clashes of class or group interest; all participants benefit from the market and therefore all their interests are in harmony. But the matter changes drastically, Mises points out, when we move to the intervention of government. For that very intervention necessarily *creates* conflict between those classes of people who are benefited or privileged by the State, and those who are burdened by it. These conflicting classes created by State intervention Mises calls *castes*. As Mises states:

> Thus there prevails a solidarity of interests among all caste members and a conflict of interests among the various castes. Each privileged caste aims at the attainment of new privileges and at the preservation of old ones. Each underprivileged caste aims at the abolition of its disqualifications. Within a caste society there is an irreconcilable antagonism between the interests of the various castes.

In this profound analysis Mises harkens back to the original libertarian theory of class analysis, originated by Charles Comte and Charles Dunoyer, leaders of French *laissez-faire* liberalism in the early nineteenth century.

But Mises has a grave problem; as a utilitarian, indeed as someone who equates utilitarianism with economics and with the free market, he has to be able to convince *everyone*, even those whom he concedes are the ruling castes, that they would be better off in a free market and a free society, and that they too should agitate for this end. He attempts to do this by setting up a dichotomy between "short-run" and "long-run" interests, the latter being termed "the rightly understood" interests. Even the short-run beneficiaries from statism, Mises asserts, will lose in the long run. As Mises puts it:

> In the short run an individual or a group may profit from violating the interests of other groups or individuals. But in the long run, in indulging in such actions, they damage their own selfish interests no less than those of the people they have injured. The sacrifice that a man or a group makes in renouncing some short-run gains, lest

they endanger the peaceful operation of the apparatus of social cooperation, is merely temporary. It amounts to an abandonment of a small immediate profit for the sake of incomparably greater advantages in the long run.

The great problem here is: why *should* people always consult their long-run, as contrasted to their short-run, interests? Why is the long-run the "right understanding"? Ludwig von Mises, more than any economist of his day, has brought to the discipline the realization of the great and abiding importance of *time preference* in human action: the preference of achieving a given satisfaction now rather than later. In short, everyone prefers the shorter to the longer run, some to different degrees than others. How can Mises, as a utilitarian, say that a lower time preference for the present is "better" than a higher? In brief, some moral doctrine beyond utilitarianism is necessary to assert that people *should* consult their long-run over their short-run interests. This consideration becomes even more important when we consider those cases where government intervention confers great, not "small," gains on the privileged, and where retribution does not arrive for a very long time, so that the "temporary" in the above quote is a long time indeed.

Mises, in "The Clash of Group Interests," tries to dismiss war between nations and nationalisms as senseless, at least in the long run. But he does not come to grips with the problem of national boundaries; since the essence of the nation-State is that it has a monopoly of force over a given territorial area, there is ineluctably a conflict of interest between States and their rulers over the size of their territories, the size of the areas over which their dominion is exercised. While in the free market, each man's gain is another man's gain, one State's gain in territory is necessarily another State's loss, and so the conflict of interest over boundaries are irreconcilable—even though they are less important the fewer the government interventions in society.

Mises's notable theory of classes has been curiously neglected by most of his followers. By bringing it back into prominence, we have to abandon the cozy view that all of us, we *and* our privileged rulers alike, are in a continuing harmony of interest. By amending Mises's theory to account for time preference and other problems in his "rightly understood" analysis, we conclude with the still less cozy view that the interests of the State privileged and of the rest of Society are at loggerheads. And further, that only moral principles beyond utilitarianism can ultimately settle the dispute between them.

THE CLASH OF GROUP INTERESTS

I

To APPLY THE TERM "group tensions" to denote contemporary antagonisms is certainly a euphemism. What we have to face are conflicts considered as irreconcilable and resulting in almost continual wars, civil wars, and revolutions. As far as there is peace, the reason is not, to be sure, love of peace based on philosophical principles, but the fact that the groups concerned have not yet finished their preparations for the fight and, for considerations of expediency, are waiting for a more propitious moment to strike the first blow.

"The Clash of Group Interests" was originally published in *Approaches to National Unity: A Symposium,* edited by Lyman Bryson, Louis Finkelstein, and Robert M. MacIver (New York: Harper and Brothers, 1945). This symposium volume was from the fifth annual meeting of the Conference on Science, Philosophy, and Religion in Their Relation to the Democratic Way of Life, held at Columbia University.

In fighting one another, people are not in disagreement with the consensus of contemporary social doctrines. It is an almost generally accepted dogma that there exist irreconcilable conflicts of group interests. Opinions differ by and large only with regard to the question, which groups have to be considered as genuine groups and, consequently, which conflicts are the genuine ones. The nationalists call the nations (which means in Europe the linguistic groups), the racists call the races, and the Marxians call the "social classes," the genuine groups. But there is unanimity with regard to the doctrine that a genuine group cannot prosper except to the detriment of other genuine groups. The natural state of intergroup relations, according to this view, is conflict.

This social philosophy has made itself safe against any criticism by proclaiming the principle of polylogism. Marx, Dietzgen, and the radicals among the representatives of the "sociology of knowledge" teach that the logical structure of mind is different with different social classes. If a man deviates from the teachings of Marxism, the reason is either that he is a member of a non-proletarian class and therefore constitutionally incapable of grasping the proletarian philosophy;

or, if he is a proletarian, he is simply a traitor. Objections raised to Marxism are of no avail because their authors are "sycophants of the bourgeoisie." In a similar way the German racists declare that the logic of the various races is essentially different. The principles of "non-Aryan" logic and the scientific theories developed by its application are invalid for the "Aryans."

Now, if this is correct, the case for peaceful human cooperation is hopeless. If the members of the various groups are not even in a position to agree with regard to mathematical and physical theorems and biological problems, they will certainly never find a pattern for a smoothly functioning social organization.

It is true that most of our contemporaries, in their avowal of polylogism do not go so far as the consistent Marxians, racists, etc. But a vicious doctrine is not rendered less objectionable by timidity and moderation in its expression. It is a fact that contemporary social and political science makes ample use of polylogism, although its champions refrain from expounding clearly and openly the philosophical foundations of polylogism's teachings. Thus, for instance, the Ricardian theory of foreign trade is simply disposed of by pointing out that it was the "ideological superstructure" of the class interests of the nineteenth-century British bourgeoisie. Whoever opposes the fashionable doctrines of government interference with business or of labor-unionism is—in Marxian terminology—branded as a defender of the unfair class interests of the "exploiters."

The very way in which social scientists, historians, editors, and politicians apply the terms "capital" and "labor" or deal with the problems of economic nationalism is the proof that they have entirely adopted the doctrine of the irreconcilable conflict of group interests. If it is true that such irreconcilable conflicts exist, neither international war nor civil war can be avoided.

Our wars and civil wars are not contrary to the social doctrines generally accepted today. They are precisely the logical outcome of these doctrines.

II

The first question we must answer is: What integrates those groups whose conflicts we are discussing?

Under a caste system the answer is obvious. Society is divided into rigid castes. Caste membership assigns to each individual certain

privileges *(privilegia favorabilia)* or certain disqualifications *(privilegia odiosa)*. As a rule a
man inherits his caste quality from his parents,
remains in his caste for life, and bestows his status
on his children. His personal fate is inseparably
linked with that of his caste. He cannot expect
an improvement of his conditions except through
an improvement in the conditions of his caste or
estate. Thus there prevails a solidarity of interests
among all caste members and a conflict of interests among the various castes. Each privileged
caste aims at the attainment of new privileges
and at the preservation of the old ones. Each
underprivileged caste aims at the abolition of its
disqualifications. Within a caste society there is
an irreconcilable antagonism between the interests of the various castes.

Capitalism has substituted equality under
the law for the caste system of older days. In a
free-market society, says the liberal economist,
there are neither privileged nor underprivileged.
There are no castes and therefore no caste conflicts. There prevails full harmony of the rightly
understood (we say today, of the long-run) interests of all individuals and of all groups. The
liberal economist does not contest the fact that
a privilege granted to a definite group of people

can further the short-term interests of this group at the expense of the rest of the nation. An import duty on wheat raises the price of wheat on the domestic market and thus increases the income of domestic farmers. (As this is not an essay on economic problems we do not need to point out the special-market situation required for this effect of the tariff.) But it is unlikely that the consumers, the great majority, will lastingly acquiesce in a state of affairs which harms them for the sole benefit of the wheat growers. They will either abolish the tariff or try to secure similar protection for themselves. If all groups enjoy privileges, only those are really benefited who are privileged to a far greater degree than the rest. With equal privilege for each group, what a man profits in his capacity as producer and seller is, on the other hand, absorbed by the higher prices he must pay in his capacity as consumer and buyer. But beyond this, all are losers because the tariff diverts production from the places offering the most favorable conditions for production to places offering less favorable conditions and thus reduces the total amount of the national income. The short-run interests of a group may be served by a privilege at the expense of other people. The rightly understood, *i.e.*, the long-run interests are certainly better served in the absence of any privilege.

The fact that people occupy the same position within the frame of a free-market society does not result in a solidarity of their short-run interests. On the contrary, precisely this sameness of their place in the system of the division of labor and social co-operation makes them competitors and rivals. The short-run conflict between competitors can be superseded by the solidarity of the rightly understood interests of all members of a capitalist society. But—in the absence of group privileges—it can never result in group solidarity and in an antagonism between the interests of the group and those of the rest of society. Under free trade the manufacturers of shoes are simply competitors. They can be welded together into a group with solidarity of interests only when privilege supervenes, *e.g.*, a tariff on shoes *(privilegium favorabile)* or a law discriminating against them for the benefit of some other people *(privilegium odiosum)*.

It was against this doctrine that Karl Marx expounded his doctrine of the irreconcilable conflict of class interests. There are no castes under capitalism and bourgeois democracy. But there are social classes, the exploiters and the exploited. The proletarians have one common interest, the abolition of the wages system and the establishment of the classless society of socialism. The bourgeois, on the other hand, are united in their endeavors to preserve capitalism.

Marx's doctrine of class war is entirely founded on his analysis of the operation of the capitalist system and his appraisal of the socialist mode of production. His economic analysis of capitalism has long since been exploded as utterly fallacious. The only reason which Marx advanced in order to demonstrate that socialism is a better system than capitalism was his pretension to have discovered the law of historical evolution; namely, that socialism is bound to come with "the inexorability of a law of nature." As he was fully convinced that the course of history is a continuous progress from lower and less desirable modes of social production toward higher and more desirable modes and that therefore each later stage of social organization must necessarily be a better stage than the preceding stages were, he could not have any doubts about the blessings of socialism. Having quite arbitrarily taken for granted that the "wave of the future" is driving mankind toward socialism, he believed that he had done everything that was needed to prove the superiority of socialism. Marx not only refrained from any analysis of a socialist economy. He outlawed such studies as utterly "utopian" and "unscientific."

Every page of the history of the past hundred years belies the Marxian dogma that the proletarians are necessarily internationally minded and know that there is an unshakable solidarity of the interests of the wage-earners all over the world. Delegates of the "labor" parties of various countries have consorted with one another in the various International Working Men's Associations. But while they indulged in the idle talk about international comradeship and brotherhood, the pressure groups of labor of various countries were busy in fighting one another.

The workers of the comparatively underpopulated countries protect, by means of immigration barriers, their higher standard of wages against the tendency toward an equalization of wage rates, inherent in a system of free mobility of labor from country to country. They try to safeguard the short-run success of "pro-labor" policies by barring commodities produced abroad from access to the domestic market of their own countries. Thus they create those tensions which must result in war whenever those injured by such policies expect that they can brush away by violence the measures of foreign governments that are prejudicial to their own well-being.

Our age is full of serious conflicts of economic group interests. But these conflicts are not inherent in the operation of an unhampered capitalist economy. They are the necessary outcome of government policies interfering with the operation of the market. They are not conflicts of Marxian classes. They are brought about by the fact that mankind has gone back to group privileges and thereby to a new caste system.

In a capitalist society the proprietary class is formed of people who have well succeeded in serving the needs of the consumers and of the heirs of such people. However, past merit and success give them only a temporary and continually contested advantage over other people. They are not only continually competing with one another; they have daily to defend their eminent position against newcomers aiming at their elimination. The operation of the market steadily removes incapable capitalists and entrepreneurs and replaces them by parvenus. It again and again makes poor men rich and rich men poor. The characteristic features of the proprietary class are that the composition of its membership is continually changing, that entrance into it is open to everybody, that continuance in membership requires an uninterrupted sequence of successful business operations, and that the membership is divided against itself by competition. The successful businessman is not interested in a policy of sheltering the unable capitalists and entrepreneurs against the vicissitudes of the market. Only the incompetent capitalists and entrepreneurs (mostly later generations) have a selfish interest in such "stabilizing" measures. However, within a world of pure capitalism, committed to the principles of a consumers' policy, they have no chance to secure such privileges.

But ours is an age of producers' policy. Present day "unorthodox" doctrines consider it as the foremost task of a good government to place obstacles in the way of the successful innovator for the sole benefit of less efficient competitors and at the expense of the consumers. In the predominantly industrial countries the main feature of this policy is the protection of domestic farming against the competition of foreign agriculture working under more favorable physical conditions. In the predominantly agricultural countries it is, on the contrary, the protection of domestic manufacturing against the competition of foreign industries producing at lower costs. It is a return to the restrictive economic policies abandoned by the liberal countries in the course of the eighteenth and nineteenth centuries. If people had not discarded these policies then, the marvelous economic progress of the capitalist era would never have been achieved. If the European countries had not opened their frontiers to the importation of American products—cotton, tobacco, wheat, etc.—and if the older generations of Americans had rigidly barred the importation of European manufactures, the United States would never have reached its present stage of economic prosperity.

It is this co-called producers' policy that integrates groups of people, who otherwise would consider each other simply as competitors, into pressure groups with common interests. When the railroads came into being, the coach drivers could not consider joint action against this new competition. The climate of opinion would have rendered such a struggle futile. But today the butter producers are successfully struggling against margarine and the musicians against recorded music. Present-day international conflicts are of the same origin. The American farmers are intent upon barring access to Argentinean cereals, cattle, and meat. European countries are acting in the same way against the products of the Americans and of Australia.

The root causes of present-day group antagonisms must be seen in the fact that we are on the point of going back to a system of rigid castes. Australia and New Zealand are democratic countries. If we overlook the fact that their domestic policies are breeding domestic pressure groups fighting one another, we could say that they have built up homogeneous societies with equality under the law. But under their immigration laws, barring access not only to colored but no less to white immigrants, they have integrated their whole citizenry into a privileged caste. Their citizens are in a position to work under conditions safeguarding a higher productivity of the individual's work and thereby higher wages. The nonadmitted foreign workers and farmers are excluded from enjoyment of such opportunities. If an American labor union bars colored Americans from access to its industry, it converts the racial difference into a caste quality.

We do not have to discuss the problem whether or not it is true that the preservation and the further development of occidental civilization require the maintenance of the geographical segregation of various racial groups. The task of this paper is to deal with the economic aspects of group conflicts. If it is true that racial considerations make it inexpedient to provide an outlet for the colored inhabitants of comparatively overpopulated areas, this would not contradict the statement that in an unhampered capitalist society there are no irreconcilable conflicts of group interests. It would only demonstrate that racial factors make it inexpedient to carry the principle of capitalism and market economy in its utmost consequences and that the conflict among various races is, for reasons commonly called noneconomic, irreconcilable. It would certainly not disprove the statement of the liberals that within a society of free enterprise and free mobility of men, commodities, and capital, there are no irreconcilable conflicts of the rightly understood interests of various individuals and groups of individuals.

III

The belief that there prevails an irreconcilable conflict of group interests is age-old. It was the essential proposition of Mercantilist doctrine. The Mercantilists were consistent enough to deduce from this principle that war is an inherent and eternal pattern of human relations. Mercantilism was a philosophy of war.

I want to quote two late manifestations of this doctrine. First a dictum of Voltaire. In the days of Voltaire the spell of Mercantilism had already been broken. French Physiocracy and British Political Economy were on the point of supplanting it. But Voltaire was not yet familiar with the new doctrines, although one of his friends, David Hume, was their foremost champion. Thus he wrote in 1764 in his *Dictionnaire Philosophique: "etre bon patriote, c'est souhaiter que su ville s'enrichisse par le commerce et soit puissante par les arnzes. Il est Clair qu'un pays ne peut gagner sans qu'un autre perde, et qu'il ne peut vaincre sans faire des malheureux."*[1] Here we have in beautiful French the formula of modern warfare, both economic and military. More than eighty years later we find another dictum. Its French is less perfect, but its phrasing is more brutal. Says Prince Louis Napoleon Bonaparte, the later Emperor Napoleon III: *"La quantity des merchandises qu'un pays exporte est toujours en raison directe du nombre*

---

[1] ["To be a good patriot is to hope that one's town enriches itself through commerce and is powerful in arms. It is dear that a country cannot gain unless another loses and it cannot prevail without making others miserable."—Ed.]

des boulets qu'il peut envoyer a ses ennemis, quand son honneur et sa dignity le cornmandent."[2]

Against the background of such opinions we must hold the achievements of the classical economists and of the liberal policies inspired by them. For the first time in human history a social philosophy emerged that demonstrated the harmonious concord of the rightly understood interests of all men and of all groups of men. For the first time a philosophy of peaceful human co-operation came into being. It represented a radical overthrow of traditional moral standards. It was the establishment of a new ethical code.

All older schools of morality were heteronomous. They viewed the moral law as a restraint imposed upon man by the unfathomable decrees of Heaven or by the mysterious voice of conscience. Although a mighty group has the power to improve its own earthly well-being by inflicting damage upon weaker groups, it should abide by the moral law and forego furthering its own selfish interests at the expense of the weak. The observance of the moral law amounts to

---

[2] *Extinction du Paupérisme* (Paris, 1848), p. 6. ["The quantity of goods which a country exports is always directly related to the number of bullets which it can send against its enemies with honor and dignity demanded."—Ed.]

sacrificing some advantage which the group or the individual could possibly secure.

In the light of the economic doctrine things are entirely different. There are within an unhampered market society, no conflicts among the rightly understood selfish interests of various individuals and groups. In the short run an individual or a group may profit from violating the interests of other groups or individuals. But in the long run, in indulging in such actions, they damage their own selfish interests no less than those of the people they have injured. The sacrifice that a man or a group makes in renouncing some short-run gains, lest they endanger the peaceful operation, of the apparatus of social co-operation, is merely temporary. It amounts to an abandonment of a small immediate profit for the sake of incomparably greater advantages in the long run.

Such is the core of the moral teachings of nineteenth-century utilitarianism. Observe the moral law for your own sake, neither out of fear of hell nor for the sake of other groups, but for your own benefit. Renounce economic nationalism and conquest, not for the sake of foreigners and aliens, but for the benefit of your own nation and state.

It was the partial victory of this philosophy that resulted in the marvelous economic and political achievements of modern capitalism. It is its merit that today there are living many more people on the earth's surface than at the eve of the "industrial revolution," and that in the countries most advanced on the way to capitalism the masses enjoy a more comfortable life than the well-to-do of earlier ages.

The scientific basis of this utilitarian ethics was the teachings of economics. Utilitarian ethics stands and falls with economics.

It would, of course, be a faulty mode of reasoning to assume beforehand that such a science of economics is possible and necessary because we approve of its application to the problem of peace preservation. The very existence of a regularity of economic phenomena and the possibility of a scientific and systematic study of economic laws must not be postulated a *priori*. The first task of any preoccupation with the problems commonly called economic is to raise the epistemological question whether or not there is such a thing as economics.

What we must realize is this: if this scrutiny of the epistemological foundations of economics were to confirm the statements of the

German Historical School and of the American Institutionalists that there is no such thing as an economic theory and that the principles upon which the economists have built their system are illusory, then violent conflicts among various races, nations, and classes are inevitable. Then the militarist doctrine of perpetual war and bloodshed must be substituted for the doctrine of peaceful social co-operation. The advocates of peace are fools. Their program stems from ignorance of the basic problems of human relations.

There is no social doctrine other than that of the "orthodox" and "reactionary" economists that allows the conclusion that peace is desirable and possible. Of course, the Nazis promise us peace for the time after their final victory, when all other nations and races will have learned that their place in society is to serve as slaves of the Master Race. The Marxians promise us peace for the time after the final victory of the proletarians, precisely, in the words of Marx, after the working class will have passed "through long struggles, through a whole series of historical processes, wholly transforming both circumstances and men."[3]

---

[3] Marx, *Der Bürgerkrieg in Frankreich,* ed. by Franz Pfemfert (Berlin: Politische Aktions Bibliothek, 1919), p. 54.

This is meager consolation indeed. At any rate, such statements do not invalidate the proposition that nationalists and Marxians consider the violent conflict of group interests as a necessary phenomenon of our time and that they attach a moral value either to international war or to class war.

IV

The most remarkable fact in the history of our age is the revolt against rationalism, economics, and utilitarian social philosophy; it is at the same time a revolt against freedom, democracy, and representative government. It is usual to distinguish within this movement a left wing and a right wing. The distinction is spurious. The proof is that it is impossible to classify in either of these groups the great leaders of the movement. Was Hegel a man of the Left or of the Right? Both the left wing and the right wing Hegelians were undoubtedly correct in referring to Hegel as their master. Was George Sorel a Leftist or a Rightist? Both Lenin and Mussolini were his intellectual disciples. Bismarck is commonly regarded as a reactionary. But his social-security scheme is the acme of present-day progressivism. If Ferdinand Lassalle had not been the son of Jewish parents, the Nazis would call him the first German labor leader and the founder of the German socialist party, one of their greatest men. From the point of view of true liberalism, all the supporters of the conflict doctrine form one homogenous party.

The main weapon applied by both the right and the left wing anti-liberals is calling their adversaries names. Rationalism is called superficial and unhistoric. Utilitarianism is branded as a mean system of stockjobber ethics. In the non-Anglo-Saxon countries it is, besides, qualified as a product of British "peddler mentality" and of American "dollar philosophy." Economics is scorned as "orthodox," "reactionary," "economic royalism" and "Wall Street ideology."

It is a sad fact that most of our contemporaries are not familiar with economics. All the great issues of present-day political controversies are economic. Even if we were to leave out of account the fundamental problem of capitalism and socialism, we must realize that the topics daily discussed on the political scene can be understood only by means of economic reasoning. But people, even the civic leaders, politicians, and editors, shun any serious occupation with economic studies. They are proud of their ignorance. They are afraid that a familiarity with economics might interfere with the naïve self-confidence and complacency with which they repeat slogans picked up by the way.

It is highly probable that not more than one out of a thousand voters knows what economists say about the effects of minimum wage rates, whether fixed by government decree or by labor-union pressure and compulsion. Most people take it for granted that to enforce minimum wage rates above the level of wage rates which would have been established on an unhampered labor market is a policy beneficial to all those eager to earn wages. They do not suspect that such minimum wage rates must result in permanent unemployment of a considerable part of the potential labor force. They do not know that even Marx flatly denied that labor unions can raise the income of all workers and that the consistent Marxians in earlier days therefore opposed any attempts to decree minimum wage rates. Neither do they realize that Lord Keynes's plan for the attainment of full employment, so enthusiastically endorsed by all "progressives," is essentially based on a reduction of the height of *real* wage rates. Keynes recommends a policy of credit expansion because he believes that "gradual and automatic lowering of real wages as a result of rising prices" would not be so strongly resisted by labor as any attempt to lower money wage rates.[4] It is not too bold a statement to affirm that with regard to this primordial problem the "progressive" experts do not differ from those popularly disparaged as "reactionary labor baiters." But then the doctrine that there prevails an irreconcilable conflict of interests between employers and employees is deprived of any scientific foundation. A lasting rise in wage rates for all those eager to earn wages can be attained only by the accumulation of additional capital and by the improvement in technical methods of production which this additional wealth makes feasible. The rightly understood interests of employers and employees coincide.

It is no less probable that only small groups realize the fact that the free traders object to the various measures of economic nationalism because they consider such measures as detrimental to the welfare of their own nation, not because they are anxious to sacrifice the interests of their fellow citizens to those of foreigners.

---

[4] Keynes, *The General Theory of Employment, Interest and Money* (London: Macmillan, 1939), p. 264. For a critical examination of this idea see Albert Hahn, *Deficit Spending and Private Enterprise.* Postwar Readjustments Bulletin, No. 8, U.S. Chamber of Commerce, pp. 28–29.

It is beyond doubt that hardly any German, in the critical years preceding Hitler's rise to power, understood that those fighting aggressive nationalism and eager to prevent a new war were not traitors, ready to sell the vital interests of the German nation to foreign capitalism, but patriots who wanted to spare their fellow citizens the ordeal of a senseless slaughter.

The usual terminology classifying people as friends or foes of labor and as nationalists or internationalists is indicative of the fact that this ignorance of the elementary teachings of economics is an almost universal phenomenon. The conflict philosophy is firmly entrenched in the minds of our contemporaries.

One of the objections raised against the liberal philosophy recommending a free-market society runs this way: "Mankind can never go back to any system of the past. Capitalism is done for because it was the social organization of the nineteenth century, an epoch that has passed away."

However, what these would-be progressives are supporting is tantamount to a return to the social organization of the ages preceding the "industrial revolution." The various measures of economic nationalism are a replica of the policies of Mercantilism. The jurisdictional conflicts between labor unions do not essentially differ from the struggles between mediaeval guilds and inns. Like the absolute princes of seventeenth- and eighteenth-century Europe, these moderns are aiming at a system under which the government undertakes the direction of all economic activities of its citizens. It is not consistent to exclude beforehand the return to the policies of Cobden and Bright if one does not find any fault in returning to the policies of Louis XIV and Colbert.

V

It is a fact that the living philosophy of our age is a philosophy of irreconcilable conflict and dissociation. People value their party, class, linguistic group, or nation as supreme, believe that their own group cannot thrive but at the expense of other groups, and are not prepared to tolerate any measures which in their opinion would have to be considered as an abandonment of vital group interests. Thus a peaceful arrangement with other groups is out of the question. Take for instance the implacable intransigence of Leninism or of the French *nationalism integral* or of the Nazis. It is the same with regard to domestic affairs. No pressure group is ready to renounce the least of its pretensions for considerations of national unity.

It is true that powerful forces are fortunately still counteracting these tendencies toward disintegration and conflict. In this country the traditional prestige of the Constitution is such a factor. It has nipped in the bud the endeavors of various local pressure groups to break up the economic unity of the nation by the establishment of interstate trade barriers. But in the long run even these noble traditions may prove insufficient if not backed by a social philosophy, positively, proclaiming the primacy of the interests of the Great Society and their harmony with the rightly understood interests of each individual.[5]

[5] [See, Ludwig von Mises's, *Socialism, an Economic and Sociological Analysis* (London: Jonathan Cape, revised ed., 1951), pp. 328–51, and *Theory and History, an Interpretation of Social and Economic Evolution* (New Haven, Conn.: Yale University Press, 1957), pp. 112–46, for a further development of the ideas presented in "The Clash of Group Interests." —Ed.]

On Equality and Inequality

I

THE DOCTRINE OF NATURAL LAW that inspired the eighteenth century declarations of the rights of man did not imply the obviously fallacious proposition that all men are biologically equal. It proclaimed that all men are born equal in rights and that this equality cannot be abrogated by any man-made law, that it is inalienable or, more precisely, imprescriptible. Only the deadly foes of individual liberty and self-determination, the champions of totalitarianism, interpreted the principle of equality before the law as derived from an alleged psychical and physiological equality of all men. The French declaration of the

This article was originally published in the journal *Modern Age* (Spring 1961).

rights of the man and the citizen of November 3, 1789, had pronounced that all men are born and remain equal in rights. But, on the eve of the inauguration of the regime of terror, the new declaration that preceded the Constitution of June 24, 1793, proclaimed that all men are equal *"par la nature."* From then on this thesis, although manifestly contradicting biological experience, remained one of the dogmas of "leftism." Thus we read in the *Encyclopaedia of the Social Sciences* that "at birth human infants, regardless of their heredity, are as equal as Fords."[1]

However, the fact that men are born unequal in regard to physical and mental capacities cannot be argued away. Some surpass their fellow men in health and vigor, in brain and aptitudes, in energy and resolution and are therefore better fitted for the pursuit of earthly affairs than the rest of mankind—a fact that has also been admitted by Marx. He spoke of "the inequality of individual endowment and therefore productive capacity (*Leistungsfähigkeit*)" as "natural privileges" and of "the unequal individuals (and they would not be different individuals if they were

---

[1] Horace Kallen, "Behaviorism," in *Encyclopaedia of the Social Sciences*, vol. 2 (New York: Macmillan, 1930), p. 498.

not unequal)."[2] In terms of popular psychological teaching we can say that some have the ability to adjust themselves better than others to the conditions of the struggle for survival. We may therefore—without indulging in any judgment of value—distinguish from this point of view between superior men and inferior men.

History shows that from time immemorial superior men took advantage of their superiority by seizing power and subjugating the masses of inferior men. In the status society there is a hierarchy of castes. On the one hand are the lords who have appropriated to themselves all the land and on the other hand their servants, the liegemen, serfs, and slaves, landless and penniless underlings. The inferiors' duty is to drudge for their masters. The institutions of the society aim at the sole benefit of the ruling minority, the princes, and their retinue, the aristocrats. Such was by and large the state of affairs in all parts of the world before, as both Marxians and conservatives tell us, "the acquisitiveness of the bourgeoisie," in a process that went on for centuries and is still going on in many parts of

---

[2] Karl Marx, *Critique of the Social Democratic Program of Gotha* [Letter to Bracke, May 5, 1875] (New York: International Publishers, 1938).

the world, undermined the political, social, and economic system of the "good old days." The market economy—capitalism—radically transformed the economic and political organization of mankind.

Permit me to recapitulate some well-known facts. While under precapitalistic conditions superior men were the masters on whom the masses of the inferior had to attend, under capitalism the more gifted and more able have no means to profit from their superiority other than to serve to the best of their abilities the wishes of the majority of the less gifted. In the market, economic power is vested in the consumers. They ultimately determine, by their buying or abstention from buying, what should be produced, by whom and how, of what quality and in what quantity. The entrepreneurs, capitalists, and landowners who fail to satisfy in the best possible and cheapest way the most urgent of the not-yet-satisfied wishes of the consumers are forced to go out of business and forfeit their preferred position. In business offices and in laboratories, the keenest minds are busy fructifying the most complex achievements of scientific research for the production of ever-better implements and gadgets for people who have no inkling of the theories that make the fabrication of such things possible. The bigger an enterprise is, the more it is forced to adjust its production to the changing whims and fancies of the masses, its masters. The fundamental principle of capitalism is mass production to supply the masses. It is the patronage of the masses that make enterprises grow big. The common man is supreme in the market economy. He is the customer who "is always right."

In the political sphere, representative government is the corollary of the supremacy of the consumers in the market. Office-holders depend on the voters as entrepreneurs and investors depend on the consumers. The same historical process that substituted the capitalistic mode of production for precapitalistic methods substituted popular government—democracy—for royal absolutism and other forms of government by the few. And wherever the market economy is superseded by socialism, autocracy makes a comeback. It does not matter whether the socialist or communist despotism is camouflaged by the use of aliases like "dictatorship of the proletariat" or "people's democracy" or "*Führer* principle." It always amounts to a subjection of the many to the few.

It is hardly possible to misconstrue more thoroughly the state of affairs prevailing in capitalistic society than by calling the capitalists and entrepreneurs a "ruling" class intent upon "exploiting" the masses of decent men. We will not raise the question of how the men, who under capitalism are in business, would have tried to take advantage of their superior talents in any other thinkable organization of production. Under capitalism they are vying with one another in serving the masses of less gifted men. All their thoughts aim at perfecting the methods of supplying the consumers. Every year, every month, every week something unheard of before appears on the market and is soon made accessible to the many.

What has multiplied the "productivity of labor" is not some degree of effort on the part of manual workers, but the accumulation of capital by the savers and its reasonable employment by the entrepreneurs. Technological inventions would have remained useless trivia if the capital required for their utilization had not been previously accumulated by thrift. Man could not survive as a human being without manual labor. However, what elevates him above the beasts is not manual labor and the performance of routine jobs, but speculation, foresight that provides for the needs of the—always uncertain—future. The characteristic mark of production is that it is behavior directed by the mind. This fact cannot be conjured away by a semantics for which the word "labor" signifies only manual labor.

II

To acquiesce in a philosophy stressing the inborn inequality of men runs counter to many people's feelings. More or less reluctantly, people admit that they do not equal the celebrities of art, literature, and science, at least in their specialties, and that they are no match for athletic champions. But they are not prepared to concede their own inferiority in other human matters and concerns. As they see it, those who outstripped them in the market, the successful entrepreneurs and businessmen, owe their ascendancy exclusively to villainy. They themselves are, thank God, too honest and conscientious to resort to those dishonest methods of conduct that, as they say, alone make a man prosper in a capitalistic environment.

Yet, there is a daily growing branch of literature that blatantly depicts the common man as an inferior type: the books on the behavior of consumers and the alleged evils of advertising.[3] Of course, neither the authors nor the public that acclaims their writings openly state or believe that that is the real meaning of the facts they report.

As these books tell us, the typical American is constitutionally unfit for the performance of the simplest tasks of a householder's daily life. He or she does not buy what is needed for the appropriate conduct of the family's affairs. In their inwrought stupidity they are easily induced by the tricks and wiles of business to buy useless or quite worthless things. For the main concern of business is to profit not by providing the customers with the goods they need, but by unloading on them merchandise they would never take if they could resist the psychological artifices of "Madison Avenue." The innate incurable weakness of the average man's will and intellect makes the shoppers behave like "babes."[4] They are easy prey to the knavery of the hucksters.

Neither the authors nor the readers of these passionate diatribes are aware that their doctrine implies that the majority of the nation are

---

[3] [For example, John K. Galbraith, *The Affluent Society* (Boston: Houghten Mifflin, 1958)—Ed.]

[4] Vance Packard, "Babes in Consumerland," *The Hidden Persuaders* (New York: Cardinal Editions, 1957), pp. 90–97.

morons, unfit to take care of their own affairs and badly in need of a paternal guardian. They are preoccupied to such an extent with their envy and hatred of successful businessmen that they fail to see how their description of consumers' behavior contradicts all that the "classical" socialist literature used to say about the eminence of the proletarians. These older socialists ascribed to the "people," to the "working and toiling masses," to the "manual workers" all the perfections of intellect and character. In their eyes, the people were not "babes" but the originators of what is great and good in the world, and the builders of a better future for mankind.

It is certainly true that the average common man is in many regards inferior to the average businessman. But this inferiority manifests itself first of all in his limited ability to think, to work, and thereby to contribute more to the joint productive effort of mankind. Most people who satisfactorily operate in routine jobs would be found wanting in any performance requiring a modicum of initiative and reflection. But they are not too dull to manage their family affairs properly. The husbands who are sent by their wives to the supermarket "for a loaf of bread and depart with their arms loaded with their favorite snack items"[5] are certainly not typical. Neither is the housewife who buys regardless of content, because she "likes the package."[6]

It is generally admitted that the average man displays poor taste. Consequently business, entirely dependent on the patronage of the masses of such men, is forced to bring to the market inferior literature and art. (One of the great problems of capitalistic civilization is how to make high quality achievements possible in a social environment in which the "regular fellow" is supreme.) It is furthermore well known that many people indulge in habits that result in undesired effects. As the instigators of the great anti-capitalistic campaign see it, the bad taste and the unsafe consumption habits of people and the other evils of our age are simply generated by the public relations or sales activities of the various branches of "capital"—wars are made by the munitions industries, the "merchants of death"; dipsomania by alcohol capital, the fabulous "whiskey trust," and the breweries.

This philosophy is not only based on the doctrine depicting the common people as guileless suckers who can easily be taken in by the ruses of

---

[5] Ibid., p. 95.
[6] Ibid., p. 93.

a race of crafty hucksters. It implies in addition the nonsensical theorem that the sale of articles which the consumer really needs and would buy if not hypnotized by the wiles of the sellers is unprofitable for business and that on the other hand only the sale of articles which are of little or no use for the buyer or are even downright detrimental to him yields large profits. For if one were not to assume this, there would be no reason to conclude that in the competition of the market the sellers of bad articles outstrip those of better articles. The same sophisticated tricks by means of which slick traders are said to convince the buying public can also be used by those offering good and valuable merchandise on the market. But then good and poor articles compete under equal conditions and there is no reason to make a pessimistic judgment on the chances of the better merchandise. While both articles—the good and the bad—would be equally aided by the alleged trickery of the sellers, only the better one enjoys the advantage of being better.

We need not consider all the problems raised by the ample literature on the alleged stupidity of the consumers and their need for protection by a paternal government. What is important here is the fact that, notwithstanding the popular dogma of the equality of all men, the thesis that the common man is unfit to handle the ordinary affairs of his daily life is supported by a great part of popular "leftist" literature.

III

The doctrine of the inborn physiological and mental equality of men logically explains differences between human beings as caused by postnatal influences. It emphasizes especially the role played by education. In the capitalistic society, it is said, higher education is a privilege accessible only to the children of the "bourgeoisie." What is needed is to grant every child access to every school and thus educate everyone.

Guided by this principle, the United States embarked upon the noble experiment of making every boy and girl an educated person. All young men and women were to spend the years from six to eighteen in school, and as many as possible of them were to enter college. Then the intellectual and social division between an educated minority and a majority of people whose education was insufficient was to disappear. Education would no longer be a privilege; it would be the heritage of every citizen.

Statistics show that this program has been put into practice. The number of high schools, of teachers and students multiplied. If the present trend goes on for a few years more, the goal of the reform will be fully attained; every American will graduate from high school.

But the success of this plan is merely apparent. It was made possible only by a policy that, while retaining the name "high school," has entirely destroyed its scholarly and scientific value. The old high school conferred its diplomas only on students who had at least acquired a definite minimum knowledge in some disciplines considered as basic. It eliminated in the lower grades those who lacked the abilities and the disposition to comply with these requirements. But in the new regime of the high school, the opportunity to choose the subjects he wished to study was badly misused by stupid or lazy pupils. Not only are fundamental subjects such as elementary arithmetic, geometry, physics, history, and foreign languages avoided by the majority of high school students, but every year boys and girls receive high school diplomas who are deficient in reading and spelling English. It is a very characteristic fact that some universities found it necessary to provide special courses to improve the reading skill of their students. The often passionate debates concerning the high school curriculum that have now been going on for several years prove clearly that only a limited number of teenagers are intellectually and morally fit to profit from school attendance. For the rest of the high school population the years spent in class rooms are simply wasted. If one lowers the scholastic standard of high schools and colleges in order to make it possible for the majority of less gifted and less industrious youths to get diplomas, one merely hurts the minority of those who have the capacity to make use of the teaching.

The experience of the last decades in American education bears out the fact that there are inborn differences in man's intellectual capacities that cannot be eradicated by any effort of education.

IV

The desperate, but hopeless attempts to salvage, in spite of indisputable proofs to the contrary, the thesis of the inborn equality of all men are motivated by a faulty and untenable doctrine concerning popular government and majority rule.

This doctrine tries to justify popular government by referring to the supposed natural equality of all men. Since all men are equal, every individual participates in the genius that enlightened and stimulated the greatest heroes of mankind's intellectual, artistic, and political history. Only adverse postnatal influences prevented the proletarians from equaling the brilliance and the exploits of the greatest men. Therefore, as Trotsky told us,[7] once this abominable system of capitalism will have given way to socialism, "the average human being will rise to the heights of an Aristotle, a Goethe, or a Marx." The voice of the people is the voice of God, it is always right. If dissent arises among men, one must, of course, assume that some of them are mistaken. It is difficult to avoid the inference that it is more likely that the minority errs than the majority. The majority is right, because it is the majority and as such is borne by the "wave of the future."

The supporters of this doctrine must consider any doubt of the intellectual and moral eminence of the masses as an attempt to substitute despotism for representative government.

However, the arguments advanced in favor of representative government by the liberals of the nineteenth century—the much-maligned

---

[7] Leon Trotsky, *Literature and Revolution*, R. Strunsky, trans. (London: Geroge Allen and Unwin, 1925), p. 256.

Manchestermen and champions of *laissez faire*—have nothing in common with the doctrines of the natural inborn equality of men and the superhuman inspiration of majorities. They are based upon the fact, most lucidly exposed by David Hume, that those at the helm are always a small minority as against the vast majority of those subject to their orders. In this sense every system of government is minority rule and as such can last only as long as it is supported by the belief of those ruled that it is better for themselves to be loyal to the men in office than to try to supplant them by others ready to apply different methods of administration. If this opinion vanishes, the many will rise in rebellion and replace by force the unpopular office-holders and their systems by other men and another system. But the complicated industrial apparatus of modern society could not be preserved under a state of affairs in which the majority's only means of enforcing its will is revolution. The objective of representative government is to avoid the reappearance of such a violent disturbance of the peace and its detrimental effects upon morale, culture, and material well-being. Government by the people, i.e., by elected representatives, makes peaceful change possible. It warrants the agreement of public opinion and the principles according to which the affairs of state are conducted. Majority rule is for those who believe in liberty not as a metaphysical principle, derived from an untenable distortion of biological facts, but as a means of securing the uninterrupted peaceful development of mankind's civilizing effort.

V

The doctrine of the inborn biological equality of all men begot in the nineteenth century a quasi-religious mysticism of the "people" that finally converted it into the dogma of the "common man's" superiority. All men are born equal. But the members of the upper classes have unfortunately been corrupted by the temptation of power and by indulgence in the luxuries they secured for themselves. The evils plaguing mankind are caused by the misdeeds of this foul minority. Once these mischief makers are dispossessed, the inbred nobility of the common man will control human affairs. It will be a delight to live in a world in which the infinite goodness and the congenital genius of the people will be supreme. Never-dreamt-of happiness for everyone is in store for mankind.

For the Russian Social Revolutionaries this mystique was a substitute for the devotional practices of Russian Orthodoxy. The Marxians felt uneasy about the enthusiastic vagaries of their most dangerous rivals. But Marx's own description of the blissful conditions of the "higher phase of Communist Society"[8] was even more sanguine. After the extermination of the Social-Revolutionaries, the Bolsheviks themselves adopted the cult of the common man as the main ideological disguise of their unlimited despotism of a small clique of party bosses.

The characteristic difference between socialism (communism, planning, state capitalism, or whatever other synonym one may prefer) and the market economy (capitalism, private enterprise system, economic freedom) is this: in the market economy the individuals *qua* consumers are supreme and determine by their buying or not-buying what should be produced, while in the socialist economy these matters are fixed by the government. Under capitalism the customer is the man for whose patronage the suppliers are striving and to whom after the sale they say "thank you" and "please come again." Under socialism the "comrade" gets what "big brother" deigns to give him and he is to be thankful for

---

[8] Marx, *Critique of the Social Democratic Program of Gotha.*

whatever he got. In the capitalistic West the average standard of living is incomparably higher than in the communistic East. But it is a fact that a daily increasing number of people in the capitalistic countries—among them also most of the so-called intellectuals—long for the alleged blessings of government control.

It is vain to explain to these men what the condition of the common man both in his capacity as a producer and in that of a consumer is under a socialist system. An intellectual inferiority of the masses would manifest itself most evidently in their aiming at the abolition of the system in which they themselves are supreme and are served by the elite of the most talented men and in their yearning for the return to a system in which the elite would tread them down.

Let us not fool ourselves. It is not the progress of socialism among the backward nations, those that never surpassed the stage of primitive barbarism and those whose civilizations were arrested many centuries ago, that shows the triumphant advance of the totalitarian creed. It is in our Western circuit that socialism makes the greatest strides. Every project to narrow down what is called the "private sector" of the economic organization is considered as highly beneficial, as

progress, and is, if at all, only timidly and bash-
fully opposed for a short time. We are marching
"forward" to the realization of socialism.

VI

The classical liberals of the eighteenth and nineteenth centuries based their optimistic apprecia-
tion of mankind's future upon the assumption
that the minority of eminent and honest men
would always be able to guide by persuasion the
majority of inferior people along the way leading
to peace and prosperity. They were confident
that the elite would always be in a position to
prevent the masses from following the pied pip-
ers and demagogues and adopting policies that
must end in disaster. We may leave it undecided
whether the error of these optimists consisted
in overrating the elite or the masses or both. At
any rate it is a fact that the immense majority
of our contemporaries is fanatically committed
to policies that ultimately aim at abolishing the
social order in which the most ingenious citizens
are impelled to serve the masses in the best possible way. The masses—including those called
the intellectuals—passionately advocate a system
in which they no longer will be the customers
who give the orders but wards of an omnipotent

authority. It does not matter that this economic system is sold to the common man under the label "to each according to his needs" and its political and constitutional corollary, unlimited autocracy of self-appointed office-holders, under the label "people's democracy."

In the past, the fanatical propaganda of the socialists and their abettors, the interventionists of all shades of opinion, was still opposed by a few economists, statesmen, and businessmen. But even this often lame and inept defense of the market economy has almost petered out. The strongholds of American snobbism and "patricianship," fashionable, lavishly endowed universities and rich foundations, are today nurseries of "social" radicalism. Millionaires, not "proletarians," were the most efficient instigators of the New Deal and the "progressive" policies it engendered. It is well known that the Russian dictator was welcomed on his first visit to the United States with more cordiality by bankers and presidents of big corporations than by other Americans.

The tenor of the arguments of such "progressive" businessmen runs this way: "I owe the eminent position I occupy in my branch of business to my own efficiency and application. My innate talents, my ardor in acquiring the knowledge needed for the conduct of a big enterprise, my diligence raised me to the top. These personal merits would have secured a leading position for me under any economic system. As the head of an important branch of production I would also have enjoyed an enviable position in a socialist commonwealth. But my daily job under socialism would be much less exhausting and irritating. I would no longer have to live under the fear that a competitor can supersede me by offering something better or cheaper on the market. I would no longer be forced to comply with the whimsical and unreasonable wishes of the consumers. I would give them what I—the expert—think they ought to get. I would exchange the hectic and nerve-wracking job of a business man for the dignified and smooth functioning of a public servant. The style of my life and work would resemble much more the seigniorial deportment of a grandee of the past than that of an ulcer-plagued executive of a modern corporation. Let philosophers bother about the true or alleged defects of socialism. I, from my personal point of view, cannot see any reason why I should oppose it. Administrators of nationalized enterprises in all parts of the world and visiting Russian officials fully agree with my point of view." There is of course, no more sense in the self deception of these capitalists and entrepreneurs than in the daydreams of the socialists and communists of all varieties.

VII

As ideological trends are today, one has to expect that in a few decades, perhaps even before the ominous year 1984, every country will have adopted the socialist system. The common man will be freed from the tedious job of directing the course of his own life. He will be told by the authorities what to do and what not to do, he will be fed, housed, clothed, educated, and entertained by them. But, first of all, they will release him from the necessity of using his own brains. Everybody will receive "according to his needs." But what the needs of an individual are, will be determined by the authority. As was the case in earlier periods, the superior men will no longer serve the masses, but dominate and rule them.

Yet, this outcome is not inevitable. It is the goal to which the prevailing trends in our contemporary world are leading. But trends can change and hitherto they always have changed.

The trend toward socialism too may be replaced by a different one. To accomplish such a change is the task of the rising generation.

INDEX

Absolutism, 31
advertising, evils of,
   34–35
autocracy, 31

Bismarck, 20
Bonaparte, Louis
   Napoleon, 15

caste system, 4–5, 10
castes, viii, 13
   conflicts of interest
     among, viii
   hierarchy of, 29
   privileged, viii
   underprivileged, viii
class analysis, libertarian
   theory of, ix
class conflict, theory of,
   viii

class war, Marxist
   doctrine of, 8
class, theory of, viii
Cobden and Bright, 25
Colbert, 25
Common man
   bad habits of, 36
   in Galbraith, 34 n.1
   in socialism, 35
   inferiority of, 35
   poor taste of, 36
   superiority of, 43
Comte, Charles, ix
conflict doctrine, 25
   supporters of, 20–21
conflict
   among producers, 12
   among wage earners,
     9–10
   between
     competitors, 7

international, 12
irreconcilable, vii, 1
   among class
     interests, 7
   between
     employees and
     employers, 23
   of rightly
     understood
     interests, 14
consumer sovereignty,
   30–31, 44
consumers' policy *(laissez
faire)*, 10–11
continuous progress,
   doctrine of, 8

*Declaration of the rights
of man and of the
citizen,* France 1789,
28
dictatorship of the
   proletariat, 31
Dunoyer, Charles, ix

economic growth, 32–33
economic nationalism
   4, 24
economic theory,
   ignorance of, 21, 24

economics,
   epistemological
   foundations of, 18
education
   role of, 38
   universal, in the
     United States, 38
equality
   biological, 27, 43
   of all men, natural,
     40
   under the law, 5–6,
     27

foreign trade, Ricardian
   theory of, 3
French constitution of
   1793, 28
Führer Principle, 31

Galbraith, J.K., 34
government, change of
   by peaceful means,
     42
   by revolution, 42
group interests, 2
groups
   nations, 2
   races, 2
   social classes, 2

Hegel, 20
high school,
    deterioration of in the
    United States, 39–40
historical evolution, law
    of, 8
Hume, David 15, 42

ideas, erroneous, vii
individual endowment,
    inequality of, in Marx,
    28
interests
    clan, vii
    group, vii
    harmony of, xi
    long-run ix, 17
    rightly understood,
        ix, xi, 23, 26
            harmony
                among, 16
    short-run ix, 17

Keynes, J.M., 22

labor unions, 13
labor, productivity of, 32
leftism, dogmas of, 28
Lenin, 20
liberalism, French *laissez
    faire,* ix

logic, Aryan, 3

Madison Avenue, evils
    of, 34
majority, guidance of by
    the elite, 46
majority, infallibility of,
    41
Marxism, 2, 7, 8, 9, 19,
    28, 44
        class conflict in, 7
mercantilism, 11–12, 24
        as philosophy of
            war, 15
mercantilist doctrine,
    14–16
        and war, 14–15
mind, logical structure
    of, 2
minimum wage rates,
    22–23
minority rule, 42
Mises, Ludwig von, as a
    utilitarian, ix
moral law, as an imposed
    restraint, 16
Mussolini, 20

natural law, doctrine of,
    27
nature vs. nurture, 38, 40

New Deal, 47

Packard, Vance, 34
Polylogism, 3
pressure groups, 12, 13
producers. *See* conflicts
producers' policy
(protectionism), 11–12
proprietary class, 10
changing
membership in, 10
protectionism
in agricultural
nations, 12
in industrial nations,
12

rationalism, revolt
against, 20
representative
government, 31
liberal theory of, 42
ruling class, vii
Russian revolution,
43–44
socialism vs. capitalism,
44

socialism, attitude of
business leaders to,
47–49
sociology of knowledge,
2
status society, 29
superior men, role of
in status societies,
30
under capitalism, 30

tariffs, 6–7
Trotsky, Leon, 41

upper classes, corruption
of, 43
utilitarian ethics and
economics, 18
utilitarianism, ix, 17

Voltaire, 15

wage earners
solidarity of interests
among, 9
See also conflicts
war, moral value of, 20

About the Mises Institute

THE LUDWIG VON MISES INSTITUTE was founded in 1982 as the research and educational center of classical liberalism, libertarian political theory, and the Austrian School of economics.

It serves as the world's leading provider of educational materials, conferences, media, and literature in support of the tradition of thought represented by Ludwig von Mises and the school of thought he enlivened and carried forward during the twentieth century, which

has now blossomed into a massive international movement of students, professors, professionals, and people in all walks of life.

It seeks a radical shift in the intellectual climate as the foundation for a renewal of the free and prosperous commonwealth. It is the mission of the Mises Institute to place human choice at the center of economic theory, to encourage a revival of critical historical research, and to advance the Misesian tradition of thought through the defense of the market economy, private property, sound money, and peaceful international relations, while opposing government intervention as economically and socially destructive.

The Mises Institute has 350-plus faculty members working with it on one or more academic projects. With their help, and thousands of donors in 50 states and 80 foreign countries, the Institute has held more than 1,000 teaching conferences, including the Mises University, and seminars on subjects from monetary policy to the history of war, as well as international and interdisciplinary Austrian Scholars Conferences.

You can visit us at Mises.org. You can subscribe to our services. You will find an extensive book catalog that includes this title, with discounts on volume purchases.

We welcome your support of our work.

www.ingramcontent.com/pod-product-compliance
Lightning Source LLC
Chambersburg PA
CBHW060000300526
45794CB00003B/1019